Former Possessions
of the Spanish Empire

November 2019

Former Possessions
of the Spanish Empire

MICHELLE PEÑALOZA

[signature]

For Patrick —
So wonderful to meet &
read with you! Thank you
for the "pick a number"
game and also your
beautiful, funny, many poems.

Inlandia Books

[signature]

Published by Inlandia Institute
Riverside, California
www.InlandiaInstitute.org
First Edition

Also by Michelle Peñaloza

landscape/heartbreak
Last Night I Dreamt of Volcanoes

for my mother and father

for my family:
blood, ghost, and chosen

CONTENTS

tatlo / three

FORMER POSSESSIONS OF THE SPANISH EMPIRE

People name us
with the separation of their teeth,
the long z of our naming.

It used to be
we were named for our proximity:
kato tabing dagat, the parentage of the sea;
the forest's lineage, kato ginubatan.

Or we were named for our parents—
anak ni Lina, bunso ni Boyet.
The song of our names
led to the discovery of garlic
growing from our palms,
the scapes forming a second green hand.

But it was in the name of good King Philip
that songs changed to names
and the naming of names became law.

A governor general made a name for himself
with the *Catalogo de Apellidos*—
a dissemination of empire, a naming of parts
to trace and tax everyone:
whole provinces renamed with efficient alphabetical phenomena:
Padilla, Pacheco, Palma, Paz, Perez, Portillo, Puente, Peñaloza.

Still, there were names we kept to ourselves,
a shorthand between us:

windows lined with votives
jars of holy water

the papaya's
lush coral and beaded seeds
shining fish roe.

Can legacy exist in shorthand?

Papal papa
papel papaya
paalam permission
please

What are the root words
for what we simply know?

How do children born of empire
once removed

possess the history
of their naming?

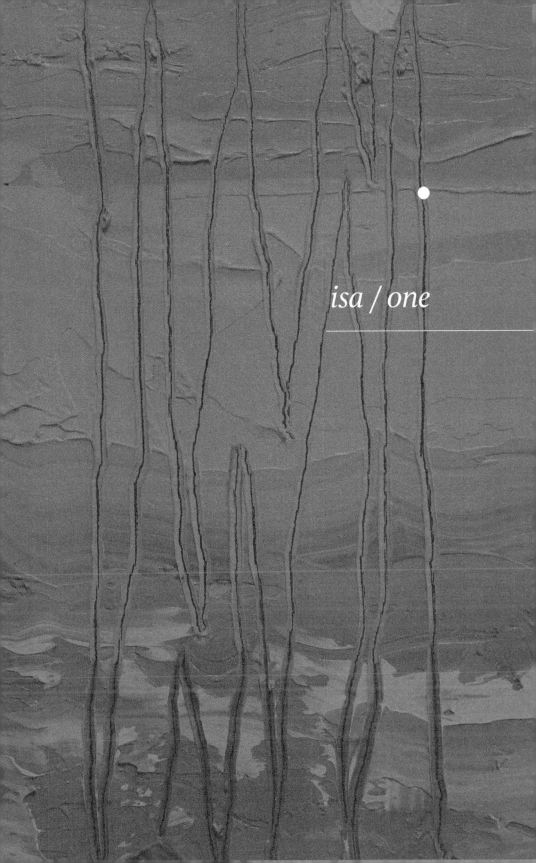

isa / one

I READ THE SIGNS

the universe says
I should trust
the moon
and scatter some faith
among the stars

my mother says
always be prepared
for the proximity of failure

she carries disappointment
like a tiny box
doling out wisdom
like an infinite gift

•

the city will shut off
our water supply
from 11pm to 7am
a paper notice announces

while we sleep
some rerouting
will siphon something
to somewhere
underground

when you sleep
and I can't
I trace the lines of your face
with my eyes

wondering about the ways
you might one day
break my heart

.

we are a people built for disappointment
for tragedy and pain

these are not lofty declarations

the ocean can attack an island from all sides
the volcano can break the earth beneath you
every single rooftop can be safe to walk on
if your whole world is buried in lahar

LETTER FROM MY MOTHER

Dear Bunso: Fall settled in the backyard today.
I finally turned on the heat inside the house—
it gets so drafty—maybe I should get someone
to seal the windows? Maybe you can do it
next time you visit? The green herons have stopped
visiting my pond and the cattails you broke apart
this summer are gone. The maples, though, they
look like they're on fire. I was single the first time
I saw fall, you know. Single and newly arrived.
So many leaves, so many new colors of leaves.
Did I tell you? Wowie's planning a fall wedding.
She's picked the bridesmaids' dresses (I hope you like
orange). Be nice. Don't complain to your cousin.
Maybe you and Alex should start some planning.
Fall is a fine time. Did I ever tell you the time
Daddy took me on a hayride? He picked the fallen oak
and maple leaves from my hair. I think we carved
pumpkins that day. I know we drank warm cider
under a cold sun. Anak, that day, like a postcard.
I went to Meijer today. They had pumpkins for sale
and a deal on apple cider—2 gallons for $4.
I bought some mulling spices for you. Kumain ka ba?
Have you been eating? What did you make Alex for dinner?
Remember: be patient and kind. Even though you aren't
married, love is all kindness and patience (Daddy—
always that way). Have you bought any pumpkins?
Maybe I'll buy one for myself this year. I haven't
carved a pumpkin since you were a little girl.
Lately I've thought: A decade is a long and not long time.
I'm getting old. I feel it when I climb the stairs before bed.
But, don't worry. I go on walks. I did some Tai Chi yesterday.
Maybe show me how to yoga when you come home
for Christmas. You still have a lot to learn from me;
what I know fills books. That's what they say, right?
You could write about me, about things that happen to me.

I'll send you poem ideas. The other day a bird with a
snake in its mouth crashed into the Blazer's windshield!
Talk about symbolism. You should write a poem about that.
Or your cousin Andrew, who's too stubborn to speak,
or Lola and Daddy—you should write poems about them.
Oh, I know what you'll say—they're dead, Ma,
let them be dead. But you're more like me than you'd like.
I'll be glad for you to come home, Bunso.
For now, I'll watch Dancing with the Stars
with your Tita Nora. Watch for the birds that are left.

BUTIKI

I cannot sleep.
My only companions:
creek of acacia beams,
moon-silence,
colloquy of gecko feet.

Legs and tails
make letters, then
words
along the walls, across
the ceiling,
constellations of sounds—
puso   usok
   aral   mahal
      —above my mosquito net,
a sky
of wiry scrawl.

Lolo told me
fallen lizards
were stars
of forgotten words that grew
tails. Light gave way
to skin, then limbs—
nimble, crawling.

Look, he said,
between nets of tilapia,
your Lola's kalán.
Look, stars inside the husk of bigas,
within kalamansi halved,
its clean tart.

Moon or not, I still call—
butiki, butiki

flit your cold-blooded feet,
walk fast, melt
across my skin.
Crawl
into my careless mouth.

THREAD RITE

I pluck silver and white hairs from Lola's head,
each one for a penny,
as she sits at her Singer.
Bridesmaids' dresses and wedding gowns
drape from the ceiling,
down from hooks meant for hanging plants.

Sundays, beneath Santo Niño and Santa Maria,
beneath the flaming, thorned heart of Christ,
Lola and I and her altars and her trilling Singer.
She pieces together lined panels of gowns
while I pull triplets of silver and white from thick black.

Triplets of silver and white, easy to find in the altar light.
Her hair smells like simmering sinigang.
She and Ma whisper fierce, below Santo Niño's painted eyes,
words I do not know.
I will buy a jawbreaker with the pennies Lola will pay me.

I don't remember their words, only their cross faces.
Their mouths move quick, twisting in ire;
these faces, someday, my mother and I will make.
We will twist our mouths, angry lines stifled—
saying and not saying what we mean.

Lola hums.
White and silver hairs gather on satin—
ruby, coral, cerulean—
leftover from finished gowns.
My fingertips massage her crown.
Lola hums a song from her throat to her skull to my fingers.

Each errant hair I pluck: a line in a sketch in a dream
where we divine patterns upon red shantung.
The song she will sing. The room where she will die.

Ma will ask everything aloud. Lola will not answer.
We wait for thread and needle, for the Singer, for satin
and sinigang, for shears.

We watch her confusion during dialysis.
Ma and I whisper fierce in the midst of her begging.
Lola asks me to pluck her weak bones, her kidneys.
She will pay me with pennies taken from mason jars.
I sit with her—each time she is sewn, pieced together,
needles going in and out,
as Santo Niño and unfinished wedding dresses watched.

Each hair a line we divined in a sketch in a dream—
a path leading, a cord binding, a rope to pull,
a sheet to cover, a handkerchief to wipe blood and tears.
Ma's triplets of silver and white multiply each time I see her.
I pluck her silver and white hairs, each one for a penny.

Q&A

Who would invent the egg?

A god with patience and a sense of wonder.

What happens to a wolf on pavement?

A wolf grows angry at hard inconvenience. A wolf scratches
until the pads of his feet bleed. A wolf does not howl on pavement.

Have you ever unfolded the moon?

Once, in a field of houseplants, I folded and unfolded the moon
like origami. The moon as frog. The moon as cup and bell and crane.

Why does your mother cry when you speak?

She has only ever leaned out of windows, leaned into the street,
into the space between the room she never left and the street
where I ran and ran and ran and ran and ran and ran away.

Have you ever screamed into a jar?

Yes.

What color was your scream?

Iridescent ecru of a broken shell. The pink granite of headstones.
Worn hoodie, heather grey. Fresh oxtail, marbled red.
The streak of ash. The phone's cold glow. The mutt's brindled coat.

Jar and jars and jars.

VESTIGE

The creak of pews makes my knees ache,
my palms and fingertips kiss.
Phosphorus, censers, old mahogany,
boxed wine, candle wax
work me like the itches
of an old collared jumper.
Worship seeps from memory to body.
I confess to the air.
Forgive me, Air, I cannot believe.
It has been three years since my last quiet.
I hold a rosary, count its beads
like the redolent string of rose petals
my Lola held close when she died.
After prayer, the attar melded with the garlic
bouquet of her hands, bulbous
scents cradling, caressing my face.
I roll each pressed round between
my forefinger and thumb, keep count:
my guilt, my guilt, my doubt—
I am not free. I cup the tangled strand,
pass it between my hands. The attar
now lives in the leaf creases of my palms.
The quiet whispers, scent is memory's companion.
I inhale calla lilies, yeast of Eucharist,
and my mother's undulating voice
wailing the Rosary at my Lola's funeral.
My mother looked like artwork then,
something of Bernini's—her ecstasy carved
into relief by her pain.
I remember cathedral light washed her face.

I envied the faith she found, her ravished heart.
Once, an old man spoke to me of faith
in dishes. How he held, washed, and dried
each dish as though it were a child in his sink—
the dishes themselves, and the fact that I am here
washing them, are miracles. I count the day's
miracles: the sweet butter on wheat toast,
the abundance of coffee, the predictability of doors,
opening and closing. The stars held within an apple,
the sound of eight separate rivers
converged in one spot, working in one measure.
Rosaries and rose petals and garlic.
Vinegar and incense and wine.

LATE AFTERNOON WITH CHAGALL

Their dotted trails—the bee, the dragonfly—loop words
with the lush buzz of pollen sprigs;
a golden cursive across the air
spelling
  fire and *chrysanthemum*—

or perhaps
they carry,
one on each wing,
   clementine and *living*,
  echo and *lodestone*—
words humming new dichotomies with every hover and flap—

the sin of spring is this: evanescence
   caught in the fervor of its newness—
  snapped like the strings of a violin,
an amplitude diminished by bolder life:
  the green leaves which overtake the flowers too soon,

leaves which unfurl
  into women, brides, flying out over the marketplace,
over baskets of berries, beet bundles, green stalks of leeks—
these women point from the sky, naming the merchants below,
  the mortals who ask,
   What rift is it that joins us?

The answer is in
etching and in *prayer*,
    in *mirth* and *collarbone*—
in the simplicity
of cello turned goat, turned rooster, turned uncle on a roof
all traveling beneath the dream of a rich, yolk-colored sun.

    What threshold brings us to this truth?

The answer is a town
disobeying gravity—cattle and figures of scripture,
    our daily bread,
walking with invisible wings:
        chrysanthemum and *fire*,
a golden cursive across the air.

VARIATIONS ON PRAYER
AND THE COLOR BROWN

My mother sends emails
telling me to be happy and grateful,
reminding me of the day's saint, instructing me
to pray the rosary and how to.
There are differing views
on origin and history—
did the Virgin Mary give Saint Dominic
a strand of beads in a vision?
Or did people simply make a way
to count their prayers?

•

My lola had visions
of Saint Anthony of Padua—
patron saint of lost items and souls;
of native peoples, amputees, animals,
of barrenness, of Brazil and Cebu;
patron saint of counter-
revolutionaries and the elderly,
of fishermen, of harvests and horses,
of poor and oppressed peoples; of Portugal
and pregnancy; patron saint of shipwrecks,
starvation, swineherds, travelers, and runts—
he appeared to my lola in the midst of her prayers.
His arrival shook the nipa roof. In his benevolent
presence, my lola pled for Saint Anthony to save
my Tito Ubing from the illness which the doctor
(they could not afford) could neither name nor cure.
She placed cold towels on her son's head
while she praised Saint Anthony for his sermon
to the fish in Rimini—a multitude in peaceful, perfect order

rose up, smallest to largest, lifting their heads out of the water
to gaze upon his face. Lola praised Saint Anthony
for converting the heretics of Remini with the miracle
of penitent fish and called on him—Doctor of the Church,
fish-whisperer, heretic-hammer, bearer of brown habit
and three-knotted cord, Anthony of Padua—to save her son.
And he did. And my lola, my beautiful lola, whose skin
sang against fabrics of coral and pink and cerulean and
ruby and jade and chartreuse and indigo and gold
pledged to renounce all color for the rest of her life,
to demonstrate her devotion. This was always
my mother's answer when I asked her:
Ma, why does Lola only ever wear brown?

•

Variants of Brown, according to Wikipedia:
AMBER, BEAVER, BEIGE, BRONZE, BUFF,
BURGUNDY, BURNT SIENNA, CAMEL, CHESTNUT,
CHOCOLATE, COFFEE, COCOA BROWN, COPPER,
COYOTE, DESERT SAND, ECRU, FALLOW, FAWN,
FIELD DRAB, KHAKI, LION, LIVER, MAHOGANY,
RAW UMBER, RUSSET, RUST, SAND, SEAL BROWN,
SEPIA, SIENNA, SMOKEY TOPAZ, TAN, TAUPE,
TAWNY, UMBER, WENGE, WHEAT.

•

When I was born, my lola could not believe
how dark I was, how dark brown—*parang*

itim!—almost black, she supposedly said.
Even in her love, what she spoke was her fear,
that darkness would mar me, that likeness
to blackness was a matter of concern, enough for
exclamation and, later, prayer. She gave me
an ironic (or hopeful?) nickname:
Mochiko, after the sweet white rice flour
she used to make palitau, housed in a thin, white box,
marked by a single blue star and red writing.

●

If I look at my hands, my arms, my face in the mirror—
I might name my hue SAND in the fall,
CAMEL or LION in the winter,
COPPER and SEPIA in spring,
SEAL BROWN in summer.

●

Lola long dead, I still enter her old room
and find her rosary made from pressed rose petals.
I cradle it in my palms, perfuming
my hands with her prayers.
I don't pray. I just wonder
at the fragrance a brown bead can hold,
how many petals, how many roses,
to make just one bead.

FAMILY KUNDIMAN

Song crossed our threshold after the war—
face veiled, body battered—carried by our Tatay.
Song's stewards followed, ang Hapón ibinigay:
three wounded pianos, soundboards scarred.
Tatay coaxed keys and tuning pins, nursed
strings and worn dampers to life. Tatay
bade us play, till he wept for our Inay,
then, he lifted Song's veil and kissed her.
What did we know of that war or his tears?
We only knew what the timber remembered:
Humming hornbeam and carved cariñosa;
love sung low through open window. Here,
within wing-shaped wood, his harana
and toil: her veil, flapping like surrender.

WE ARE SO SORRY FOR YOUR LOST

We sort the cards at the kitchen table.
Instead of flowers our people help
the family pay for the funeral.
My mother and aunt document
the names and amounts of money in each envelope.
Silent clerks of the economics of condolence.
I alone read the short scrawls of sympathy.
Inside a card covered with lilies, someone writes
We are so sorry for your lost.
My uncle has lost his wife.
No. My uncle's wife has died. No.
My aunt passed away. No.
My aunt died. She died
in the summer, in a season of gunpowder,
succumbed to fire in her lungs and stomach
and throat and everywhere.
This scrawl makes more sense
than anything else anyone's written
inside a sympathy card.
Our dead are lost, aren't they?
There is always some mistake:
lost down a well, lost in the woods.
Lost for words, lost to the world,
we'll never make up for lost time.
The sheep, the baby, the prodigal son,
wandering beyond our imaginings,
along the border of our grief and need.

NIGHT FISHING

Unpainted, this night's song.
One of fishermen's hands and nets,
numinous, numerous as the nets for thought:
nimble, light casting without lead sinkers;
loose-woven, the widest mesh for use in swamps;
dragnets for the shallow water; nets like sieves
for quick catch in surf; immense nets, set
upright between boat's edge and shore
to catch fish leaping high into night's air,
hungry for torch flames above the water;
nets that fasten to the small of a fisherman's back,
like the belt of a weaver wielding a backstrap loom.
A bright dance of petals beneath this inky water:
kindled scales, buoyed closer and closer,
breathe with the waves.

The old fishermen tell stories of fish
who surfaced, breathing above the water,
spawned in the roots of mangrove trees.
The older fishermen tell stories of men,
sweet-scented with civet or ambergris,
painted like lizards or birds of prey;
they asked the fish, one by one.
Leave the shoal, climb trees.

The silver fish sidle inshore,
opaque lines, nets of the mind—
words before they leave the tongue.
The torches their lures,
the old men watch the clamor of fish
climb the branches of their swaying nets.

TO THE OLDER COUPLE ALSO EATING DUNKIN' DONUTS AT O'HARE

For eavesdropping while I said goodbye
to my already-calling mother, already worrying

across the 239 miles from Detroit. For your questions,
for looking at my left hand and asking me my age.

For asking about my parents' hometowns and combing through
your family trees to find a great-aunt who married a Peñaloza.

You looked for our kinship in San Pablo and in tongue. Thank you
for marveling as I strung together the beads of one continuous strand,

from me to my mother to you both. Thank you
for your confession: your grandchildren can't understand,

nor remember a word you teach them. I'm sorry—
I've forgotten your names. Maybe I found it easier

to believe my mother from Bulacan and nothing else brought us
to these tables as we waited for our connections from O'Hare—

your distant cousins in Malolos, my father from Laguna.
You drank coffee, your crow's-feet peeking over white styrofoam;

both of you made me crave the embrace my father might give me,
the goodbyes that he and my mother might repeat if

together they'd seen me off in Detroit and waited for me to board
my plane to Seattle. For choosing sugar and orange poured-plastic

seating, your trip to Dallas-Fort Worth and our kinship in blood—
I give you my name over shared coffee and crullers.

I give you how I might look at your age;
I give you your next connecting flight.

NOSTALGIA IS A DANGEROUS THING

If you're an immigrant child,
nostalgia is your sibling.
I am an only child and still
this must be true.
Phantom sister, brother specter:
my mother gave birth to you a million times.
Each time she answered the question,
"Where are you from?"
Each of my mispronunciations inherited, each forgotten word,
each *that was a long time ago*.
        My mother used to kill chickens.
The oldest girl, she was tasked with slicing open
each de-feathered neck, carefully and slowly,
collecting all the blood to season the rice they'd eat for dinner.
        My mother has never asked me to kill a chicken.
Not once. My mother, in the scheme of things, asks for little.
At most, I am tasked with simply coming home
and even then I fail.
Nostalgia makes home hard
to find. I have grown so far from the stories my mother tells
that movies are closer.
A League of Their Own or *Don't Tell Mom
the Babysitter's Dead*, movies I watch over and over again,
not on purpose but because they're on
and even though I've seen them a million times, I cannot
bring myself to change the channel.
I could sing their scripts in my sleep.
If only I could screen my mother's plotlines
like they're fiction,
created and produced by some studio,
recorded with the swelling music and golden lighting
of wistful remembrance made to make me
feel like I could feel them, like they could be mine.

dalawa / two

TRANSGRESSION

Dogeater Dirty
Chinks Eat Dogs—

Swallow
the memory of this:
moving as one,
a school of children,
playing at protecting Coco,
Lassie, and Bud from your sloe-eyed
hunger, your starving teeth.

Savor. Swallow.
Adobong aso tasted mild,
like tender sweet beef
stewed with garlic, peppercorns,
and bayleaf singing on your tongue.
Banaue's terraces
and distant house lights glowed
while the night grew watery
and warm with a man's whispers.
Mirrors of paddy-water reflected his eager voice
and the moon, which asked:
Did the sea ever spread itself across this height?
Did the brine leave fish in the soil?
Did the fish leave bright roe shining in the water?

His voice clasped
your ear like the husks
that hold unreaped bigas.
You are *mabait* and *beautiful*.
He turned you. *Kind* and *maganda*.

Let the moon, let possibility
linger. Wouldn't it be—
meat still on your breath, his face
between your breasts, your legs
open to this vista, your brown bodies
striking, echoed across landscape—
would it wake the land's bones, the ocean
waiting beneath the fertile soil?

You will remember this moment as a lie.
Waiting with him. Watching the terraces
gleam like a school of fish
as your bus to Manila arrived.
He asked, knowing the answer:
Your husband—puti?
You boarded your bus, nodding,
yes, white.

"PATTERNS OF LOVE IN PEOPLE OF DIASPORA"

after Li-Young Lee

As a child I swallowed my sorrow,
a swelling of invisible wings

syrup-sweet, stuck
fluttering in my throat—

"I want to sing, but I don't know any songs."
Against the softest parts of us,

scales of sharps and flats swarm
a music that lives inside the skull.

How to free this buzzing in the mind
in the mouth:

when I say, "My father played the piano
from memory, but could read no notes at all,"

I mean, "I love you." When I say,
"He told me, a key change is

an opening, a sweetness, a hollow in the throat."
I mean to say, "And now. Say you love me back."

PIONEER

The mythifying process can [alter] its object beyond recognition.
—Bernard Heuvelmans

I have had many men
profess to me
their love
of my people.

The first boy I ever let
touch me
marveled
at the difference in
our skin,
my hairlessness, my
taut brown.
His eyes wide, I felt
his white
hands spread me open
as he whispered to someone else
in the room: *I knew
she would be tight.*

MAGSAYSAY DRIVE, OLONGAPO CITY: NA WALA SA PAGSASALIN

1 sa simula: in the beginning
   Malakas and Maganda
   looked over the mountains
   frolicked in the bay—
   their hair smelled
   of sampaguita
   and bougainvillea

   ngayon people come
   to Subic   Bay
   dive among the wrecks
   of Spanish galleons
   Japanese   hell ships

   treasure hunters
   GIs   preachers
   tourists   all come
   to Magsaysay Drive

2   neon buzzes
            streets alive
        HOT LIPS   TOP GUN
        RED ROOSTER
        Open   Girls Girls Girls

        inside bars
        school jumpers traded
        for tight dresses
        now slack   with wear

        the girls   slip
        sampaguita
        behind their ears—
        scent   travels even
        in dark

        in ether
        foreign faces   circle
        mirrored stages

        overseas   gazes
        sun in sprinkled
        refraction   disco ball
        petals and sequin

3   it was Rosario's
        third time
        to a short-time motel

        later they found her
        behind the dumpster
        of Happy Bake Shop—
        smell of iron   feral matter
        soaking their clothes
        as they held her
        bleeding
        her repeating
        numbly pointing   down   there
        masakit dito

4   did you hear
        about the 12-year-old girl
        who bled to death
        a piece of vibrator   broken
        left inside her

        did you hear
        about the German tourist
        arrested for pedophilia
        he bribed local police
        to place   local children
        inside   his jail cell

        did you hear
        his life   sentence
        lasted
        two years

5   Luzviminda climbs
        154 stone stairs
        her hands brush bougainvillea
        blooms   fuchsia framing
        the Grotto of Our Lady of Pardon
        Luzviminda inhales salvation
        heavy   incense sweet

        she lights a candle
        for Rosario
        though   she doesn't know
        her name

        Luzviminda climbs home
        for kisses from mga bata
        their eyelids   drowsy petals
        wave good night—

        Luz
        what her clients call her
        is a good-time gal:
        stuffs her bra
        slips a fake flower   behind her ear

        HOT LIPS at the door
        she bums a smoke from Maganda
        prays   for deep pockets
        around the stage

6   anthers release pollen
        scintilla of cadmium yellow
        like hard-ons   promise
        scraps of money
        of means

        but ends
        move across the florid stage
        this crowded   garden
        these bright wilting flowers

        lips move
        like owls
        asking   who
        in dark corners

        pollen covers
        everything

7   Malakas and Maganda
        work Magsaysay strip
        he makes drinks
        she dances naked

        later   together
        they'll wash the smell
        of cigarette smoke
        from each other's hair

        he'll frame her face
        with bougainvillea   sampaguita

DESIRE

after Terrance Hayes

Turn your face. Face the horizon from another side
to watch the line between land and sky, upend and rise:
a schism slit view, red
and swollen. I speak of something like ire—
a sweetness that resides,
sings in the body like the reed
born from runnel, given second life in the mouth. Ser,
to be. Tú eres
mi amor: one seed
born from need, clear and dire.

WHEN MY MOTHER WAS EARTHA KITT

Along the bottom of a forgotten bankers box:
a pair of black patent stiletto boots,
knee-length, and, somehow, once my mother's.
The woman who bought these boots:
twenty and nubile, she smokes Capris
and throws back her head, laughing at off-color
men who broadcast their broken attempts
to woo in languages just as foreign to her—
konnichiwa, ni hao ma.
She is impervious and breezy and says things like,
"Now I bet you'd never try that with Julie Newmar!"
Her world, onomatopoeic: heels staccato
pounding Detroit's salt-ground pavement; men drop
their highballs of bourbon—Bam! Pow!
Kaboom!—as her slight frame slinks
past rows of wooden barstools. She purrs.
When I found those boots in the 6th grade, I knew
my own feet would never unlock their magic.
My own body monstrous and lumbering
compared to the petite contours from which I came.
I knew men would never whimper to tongue my boots.
Eartha Kitt mother, what would you say
to the woman before you today?
Would you understand your daughter's
self-fulfilling prophecies? Her need
for distance, her proclivity for
the third person. Her intoxication with
the power of a man she cannot name
emptying himself inside her,
the hollowness of his embrace.

THE FIRST

This morning I woke dreaming of a man
I'd not undressed in fifteen years.
We may as well have written letters with goose quills.
The mind's meddling, curious—why him, why now?
Still, it's fun to throw spaghetti against the wall.
See what falls, what sticks. Isn't this a game
we're always losing? The root of diminution.
Take this memory, then that. Strip a coy dream
down to dirt in your mouth, leaves scattered across the water.
My temperament then, as now, such an angry one—
hidden (or maybe not) below my need to please,
to be loved by many. What ego is this? Who bleeds
for cocktails? Strips naked for a few handshakes?
Offers her purring throat for one song of praise?

PARTIAL

Not exactly that
I didn't want it. After all,
I wore a bra out
as a shirt. I snorted half a stranger's
cocaine and ignored the cabbie
who asked my drunk ass, "You sure?
You know this guy?" Ignored
the pictures of a couple all around
what I could see
of a couple's dark apartment.
Fumbling in the dark seemed
like the right thing
to do. His dick too
limp
for fucking.

The next morning
not exactly that
I didn't want it. Only
I wasn't really awake only
I woke
to his hands pulling down
my thong
him flipping me onto
my stomach
and I thought
it was just
easier
to pretend the way
he did that
I wasn't really
there to let
my body
become a moment
let his body

weigh me
my body down until
I wasn't really
there
I never said
a word only
it wasn't
exactly
later he gave me
his band's t-shirt
to cover my tits
on the subway ride home

later I took a burning hot shower
went to brunch with friends
spoke
like a stranger
was what I wanted
like times before only
I burned
that t-shirt and even now
I tell myself
it was not

UPON READING *UNDERSTANDING THE FILIPINO*

Much can be assigned to Holy Week,
as it is known that bleeding lessens
in that season. Sacred blood at the center,
the scrapes and lacerations of the unholy
don't register in the week's taxonomies of pain.
For example, a man can crawl into a girl's
bedroom, inside her family home,
and rape her. But, it is not rape to anyone
but her. Gapang, sleep crawling. No wonder
then the house my mother made of fear,
that I never spent the night anywhere other than our home.
Ingress and egress, home and not-home,
rape and not-rape. Crawl, walk, run. Accumulation:
speck after speck, the ground slowly covered.

PROVERBIAL

With you, always an impossible math.
You brought another couple into our bed—
two's company and three's Musketeers.
So, what room did that leave for me?
Because I loved you
I welcomed them and fed them cake.
I declared how very French the whole thing felt.
Until one day, I found my place
reduced to a spot at the foot of the bed.
The takeover: hostile and chock full of imperialist overtones.
Still, I can't begin to do the calculations.
You can lead a horse to water, but
how? Am I the water?
If you lead a horse to water at 3MPH,
how long after midnight will
the giardia colonize its intestines?
Am I the horse?
The arithmetic of proverbs is what's left now:
A penny saved is not much, darling.
Spots cannot change their leopard.
A journey of one step begins with a thousand miles.

Q&A

Why did you stay?

> *My feet were ashen and he hid my shoes; I was too*
> *ashamed to leave the house.*

How did you know you loved him?

> *I'd wrap the phone cord around each of my thighs*
> *and pull the distance we spoke across*
> *on my sex, willing his mouth to echo there.*

How did you know he loved you?

> *His dancing hands left the steering wheel and somehow*
> *we kept going. He hid country roads in the private windows*
> *of his search engines. His thumbprints, on everything—*
> *the bed foam, the eggplants, the threadbare sponge,*
> *the corners of my eyes. He pressed and pressed*
> *like pressing was what his life was for.*

Why did you stay?

> *There were certain verbs I couldn't*
> *remember—leave, eat, sleep, retreat—*
> *Everything became: repeat, repeat, repeat.*

How did you leave?

> *Even when I left (my body)—I stayed.*
> *I walked in circles along a river path*
> *and marked distance by the height of the grasses*
> *until I couldn't, until the acres of green*
> *went farther than I could continue,*
> *stretching out like the sea.*

How did you leave?

Now this little, now that little. I paid
attention to accumulation. I could not stop
asking: is he a trap who doesn't know?
Is the trap who he is? Does that kind of
cruelty live inside a person's blood?

THIS IS NOT A GENTLE POEM

The larynx, pinched pliers.
The mouth a purple feather.

A circle of mushrooms, the heart;
smashed glass, the smile, littered

along chain-link. I cataloged
the world this way; that is to say,

the man I learned to unlove
taught me myself, a new blazon:

ankles as handlebars, the face
a plate to lick clean. Breasts

uncompromising as bruises.
Do I regret the breath I lost

there, the frantic skin on carpet?
I looked to his hand become a gun.

I ran away on two rusted nails, listening
to the concrete cry out beneath me.

UPON READING *THE CONFESSIONS OF ST AUGUSTINE*

We do things, like steal,
not for the objects themselves
but for the profound joy
of having procured them.
l mean to say: to steal the pears,
mealy, unripe and unsweet,
was more the joy than the pears themselves.

The first time l cheated,
the taste of another man
was not delicious.
The warmth of his ecstasy in my mouth
was not delicious, but
my betrayal was like honey.

The arc of my body, resigned
and rising at another's touch,
meant that l could never fully
be anyone's.

And that felt like life.
Made me feel alive. Restoring
all the little ways you killed me.

Our life then—was it not
a series of little murders?

The metallic scent of us, like blood
in our bed, the two of us swimming
in blood each night.

Who can say now if we ever loved each other?
Looking back, there are only sad walls.

More vivid are all the times
I escaped you:
how I loved the sordidness
of sex in places not meant for sex.
Dingy sheds, late drunken alleys—
every cliché you could never imagine.

I never told you.
All those moments had nothing
to do with love,
had everything to do with how little you loved me.

You cheated on me more times that I can count.
Still, my infidelities, each one
I kept for myself—
unripe fruit, ripening in the dark.
Savoring its eventual sweetness
and its eventual rot.

A STRANGE CONSTELLATION OF DESIRES

Because of the garden and the salt
I left there Because Billie Holiday slept there
once Because of the lentils in jars the hydrangeas drunk on pennies
the grafted apple trees the Italian plums the Rainier cherries
Because he told me he loved me Because I believed him Because
he told me I was crazy Because he made me
believe Because of the dinner parties and barbecues
and birthdays and karaoke and board games and puzzles
Because being alone meant losing Because he couldn't
brush his teeth without me Because I had nowhere
else to go Because people were coming over for dinner
and we'd already invited them weeks ago Because
I owed him and I would ruin all of his plans
Because it's not like he ever hit me Because I had
already tried so many times before Because my friends were tired
of hearing me cry so I stopped crying and I stopped having friends
who heard me cry Because I am not a quitter
Because he owned me Because no one knew Because
I loved him too Because he said I was crazy Because my hair
would fall out Because I was crazy Because of the moon
Because of my dead father Because a ghost would enter
my body and not speak with my mouth Because the mangos
would never taste right again Because of the peonies
their bowed heads heavy with dew

WHEN WILL WE ACHE LESS

From a desert in Nevada   a man launches flowers
into space

just now I thought: why   when you are closer
am I more lonely?

   (the you
         could be anyone)

maybe distance is what I equate   with love

you are away and I am   alone with the bullfrogs
and crickets and raccoons
       that pull up the new sod like carpet
their child fingers searching for
               grubs in moonlight

elsewhere white men chant
   you will not replace us

why is being born white
   in America not enough?

above me the geese form haphazard
    V   V
        V   floating over the house
loose victories each twilight
       paraded from one sewage pond
to the other across town
     they don't leave the valley for winter

  •

this world and what comes from   our garden is too much
to process

abundance is a burden of responsibility
this rash of tomatoes reappears and reappears
with so little effort   with so little to do with me

what is it like to be everywhere
    to be seen and heard and known and believed
with so little effort   so little to do with you

•

I collect facts

        facts are marbles in my mouth
how to hold each one   how to keep
how to speak how to scream with so much to contain

my mouth grows bigger and bigger

butcher birds hold their prey
and dismember it   the cacti their knife and larder

26 young Nigerian women
were fished from the Mediterranean and dried as headlines
and disappeared again

bullets shot from an AR-15   move through bodies
like boats   exits wounds the size of oranges

hyenas eat ghosts   that wander the streets
they eat the bones the butchers' sons and sons and sons
feed them from their hands

someone found a grasshopper   stuck

among van Gogh's olive trees   trapped 128 years

•

dragonflies hover over the kiddie pool we soak in   to beat the heat
thrips burnish a thousand holes into a row of bright green leaves
the scuttle of skinks along the fence line   sings feline   a rolodex of r's

                a raccoon just made
carcass   splayed across the road
            the cattle wires come alive   with feathered gargoyles
spread wings follow each speeding car
                            every hour more wings   sky-full
                                        coast on warm carrion-wind
I could measure the days this way
                            name after name after name
the raccoon   a meat balloon fur crumple
                        disappearing

            disappearing

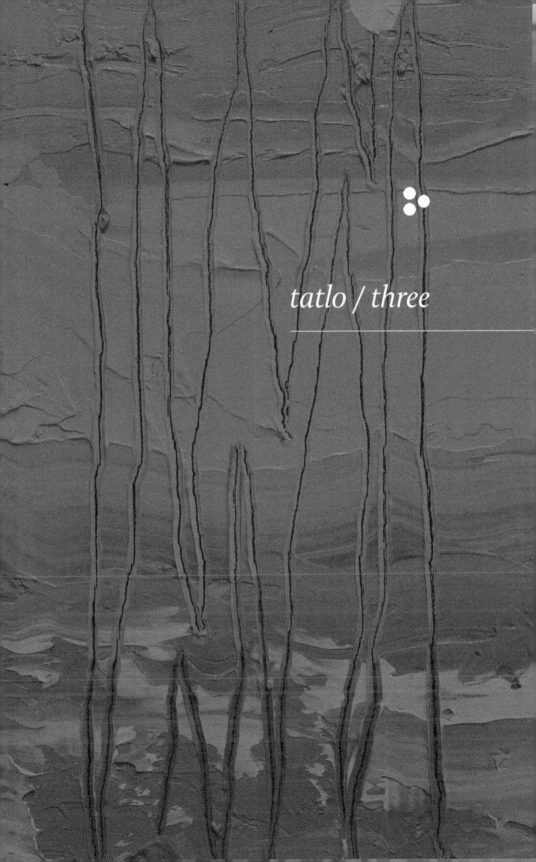

tatlo / three

ON MIGRATION, UPON FINDING AN OLD MAP

Look to a sky
   a sea
   remember
the scent of your wife's hair
       one day disappeared from the pillows
  your children grown   across the telephone's crackle
and the smallest memories
        worn by your recalling,
      traveled time zones beyond recognition.
Look to a sky
   a sea
  you've forgotten.

Hearts in red crayon and penciled dates of departure
   fade
       over Michigan's thumb and Manila

San Pablo and Jersey City
       these scratchings: artifacts of longing
     hummed outside of time's passage.

I have followed faces
      sunned by the wind
   noses elongated nightly by clothespins
names pruned of tildes
      sheared of their warbling vowels

I have followed boxes heavy with hand-me-downs
  coffee tins
   and potted meats
    box after box secured with rope and duct tape
 sent in absence
   after the crackle of distant news

I have followed time's passage

                              across yellowing landscape

        I can believe almost anything—

that we began
as thoughts an ocean away   carried as seeds or smog or trash
                                 across the water
        by capital   by will   by God
              or
we began
              as crumbs   ferried in the beaks of
                        waxwings   birds of paradise
we began
                        as birds ourselves—
        migration
                              instinct.

              Pins pierce dots and blocks of color
to yoke memory to cartography:

        we've scattered across the world.

Tiny planets
                        mark crumbs
              entire lives spun
                              along axes imperceptible
to souls never moved by the wind.

MY FATHER, ON THE LINE

He never went to the bar with Ernie, Pete and Dave
after they'd been given notice.
Once, years before,
he brought me to the factory floor—
a vast and harnessed frenzy—beginning with the body bank,
where operators assigned VIN stamps and specs,
then the line that dressed and plumbed the engines.
Men and machines were partners in an endless dance—
welding fenders, assembling brake lines and rear axles.
I ambled, my gaze following my father's:
a finished motor guided to the chassis line;
a subframe mounted onto a carrier truck, waiting
for its front suspension, steering and link.
My father waved to his buddies on the line—
he pointed to the plant's robotic limbs,
grinned at each arm securing each part into its place.
He explained—*uniting cluster and wiring, brake booster,
rear bumper and guards*—his specific labor, his line.
My father's work—didn't matter which shift—made him
happy with purpose; the rush of assembling, constant;
the outcome of completion, assured. I don't know
what he'd say about my Japanese-made car.
He did not live to see the plant close.
Now, there is only the assemblage of stories we tell.
I watched the almost-cars—subframes, rear springs
and shocks bolted up—reach the final line; chassis after chassis,
molded to body after body. My father stood beside one,
pointing with pursed lips, nudging my arm:
See, what it takes?

DAGURREOTYPE

A child waits on the sea.
He cannot explain how the water
became an endless field of bamboo,
banana leaves, rolling wild grass and fern.
Only that one night the moon
was bright enough to break his sleep.
Beneath that light, his mother became an ibis;
his father and brother, two tiger shrikes,
sister, a laughing thrush.
They flew into the moonlight,
the sea-reefs' branches of water,
unceasing waves of leaves.

Oarless and alone, the boy learned—
the leaves could power his boat with song.
They sang of creatures of the swamp,
of killing fields
and hills of poisoned trees.

The leaves carried the boy to sanctuary,
away from the fields of the sea.
There, he kept the songs
and taught himself to sing.
He sang to ibis, shrike, and thrush
songs of children who could grow wings,
songs that could conjure galaxies
in the bowls of lotus leaves,
become butterflies in his mouth.
He sang to the infinity he found: the billowing grass,
the fronds of ferns, the quicksilver of the moon.

LAVA

A river swept away a woman
who drowned in the Alaska night.

My lover offers to bring me coffee;
I cannot manage to leave our bed.

The construction around our apartment
hammers and hammers and hammers.

A poet I admire writes about minefields
and the way we dance away from terror.

I cannot manage to leave our bed. I fear
my toe touching the wood floor,

its brief expanse will somehow claim me
or the floor will become lava like it did

when we were children and either way
I will burn or burst or break if I leave this bed.

Last night I dreamt of deserts and my lover slowly
eroded like a pillar of salt left to the wind and sun.

Two women went hiking and crossed a river.
One woman crossed and the other

the river swept away. In terror
forty people searched in the night

only for a helicopter to find her body.
I played a game as a girl trying

to get to Oregon. I would always ford the river
paying no mind to the weight of my wagon

or the depth of the water.
Leading my oxen to certain doom,

I didn't yet know the duties
and payments of love.

PAYATAS

Rizal forever
gazes at the passing Pasig,
donning his bronzed bowler hat. He rivals
Niobe, seeing—*smelling*—this river reduced
to runnel, following its scent
past Malacañang to Quezon.
A place once ravine, now a city
built along tributaries of trash: Payatas,
a steaming cordillera, supporting life
atop the refuse that shapes its peak; a dumpsite
fertile with plastic bags
roiling in the mount's current of hot wind.
Every hour trucks line up:
lupa, garbage, earth, basura. The people
swim in detritus endless
as the waves that surround these islands.
They know the discarded
currency—losing lottery stubs, empty
formula tins, rice sacks, San Miguel glass.
If they close it, we'll follow the trash.
And me, a balikbayan, I've come
here to—to what? I follow my tour guide,
Boyet, the barangay captain. I enter his home,
drink his beer. We eat pulutan. Savor
fried paddy crabs balanced with kalamansi.
Before us, Payatas climbs ever higher against the sky.
There are things more foul than trash. Children, no longer
allowed on its peak, splash in a wading pool
built by Martin Sheen. Boyet shows me autographed
headshots of Marlon Brando and Dennis Hopper.
His uncle was an extra in *Apocalypse Now.*
We clink bottlenecks. *When you return*, he says,
tell people we don't want their pity.
From the mural behind us, Rizal,
ilustrado, painted and hallowed, stares
beyond us at this mountain.

HECETA BEACH

1   The pelicans paddle
     in coils of waves and light. Low tide
     reveals fissures of saltwater and rock.
     From the smallest crevices
color insists—colonies of jade
anemones, a purple starfish harvest, barnacles
hiding beaks of unbleached linen, black mussel
bouquets. Between the air and sea,
—this, one large prayer.
I kneel.

2   These rocks
        are the church
    where I knelt
        in black worsted silk
    beside my mother.
        Her shoulders sharp
    beneath my embrace.
    My mother: a solid wailing.

    These rocks are the soil
        where she kneels
    before the whorls of roses,
    keening before that box
        as if it were my father's grave.

        The closed anemones
    offer their sticky blossoms
    as the tide washes toward me.

        Small bits of the coast
    meet my skin,
        scraping my iron
            onto my knees.

3   The tide moves me
     higher on the crags. My joints crunch
     like the mussels
     and barnacles beneath my boots.
     I walk a tightrope,
     from here to another ocean
huddled with archipelagos
     where ancestral canoes
     set to paddle across the world.
     I teeter and my hands catch
     the water rising cold.
The sea we come from is much warmer.

4   How grief
      pummels us sharp,
      breaks upon us to shape
      the faces we give the world,
      the languages we speak in secret.
      Here, far above the water line
      pines congregate and meet the ocean.
      Landscape climaxes against the crash of water.
      The white walls strike
   this fawn height.

IN DREAMS, THE DEAD SING

Of this place, born of contradiction:
not sky, no angels. But ancestors and earth.
All this time, its light a riddle
below the surface,

as though the loam swallowed a star.
In the glint of this impossible light
there should be no life, yet there is
such noise. Not peace,

but noise that is peace, imperceptible
to the living: the dead throw back
their heads, their mouths drunk
with song—

the monarch emerged
from its chrysalis, the veil dropped,
the soul parted from the body.
A thin secret kept from the living,

the noise of heaven murmurs under
our fingernails, in the flaked tears
we wipe from our waking eyes,
in the dust that flocks to the corners

of all our forgotten rooms. The dead sing
within the salt dissolved on living tongues,
in the plumed mist of torn citrus peel,
the dreaming amber of honeycomb,

in concert with locusts' wings. Humming
among the taut skins of drums, the salted
wood of ocean canoes crosses the dawn.
The eyes inside all figs blink. The fern's fist

unfurls into an open palm, carrying
the quiver at the heart-center
of all the exhalations of the living.

CONSTELLATION

after Terrance Hayes

The stars above us ask so little,
despite our cells,
coursing with their dust. To err is constant—
someday, all the things we believe will seem ancient.
Perhaps, we'll live more times than once.
Eventually, we will all flee toward the coastline.
The world we ignore most and understand least
will call us back to give up our toenails for tails,
cover our breasts with starfish and numinous scales.
Tell me, how will a cellist sound beneath the sea?

TABI TABI, PO

Strange, given all my time
talking to and obsessing over the dead:
I was warned, but I didn't quite believe
in you, despite my embrace of the woo-woo.
I've got oils and sage, some totems and crystals—
but you're right to call me out.
It's all show. My heart's not been in it.
My heart, I think, is tired. Sad. Maybe a little bored?
(I know! Only boring people are bored!
And how could I be bored within such austere beauty?
And with such joyful tasks and objects—
oh, snow-covered walkway! Oh, tiny axe! Oh, bright fire!)
My bored heart speaks to something larger lost in me.
What am I doing here? In this triangle of snow, pines,
and more snow? I haven't prayed, really prayed,
in a long time and even when I do, like now,
it's only when I need something. Like, when I call my mother.
I know. A bad attender of ghosts, a bad daughter, too.
Y'know, I learned first to talk to spirits, not on this continent
but on the islands from which my parents came.
I walked through jungles in day's-end gloaming, whispering,
tabi tabi, po—excuse me, ma'am, pardon me, sir—
to the diwata and aswang and kapre and goblin and ghost
and manananggal and tikbalang and kumakatok—
to let them know I was coming. To say: I know you
are real, thank you for letting me pass. I mean no harm.
Forgive me. I never did introduce myself, never even
asked your names. You've been trying to talk to me since I got here—
sliding snow off the roof, blowing flakes into my boots
—but I've been so busy, so serious, I failed to answer
when you asked me to play. Well, I'm ready
to play and pray and so, spirits of snow, otter gods,
lichen sprites, child ghosts of the forest—Hello. *Tabi tabi, po.*

SELF-PORTRAIT AT THIRTY-THREE

Christ-aged, I thought I'd have
born a child by now. I justify
my empty wound by filling my belly,
watching myself grow fat with abundance—
the various joys of three decades and three years,
the fucks I have given and refuse
to give. My reflection sun-kissed and bare.
My face, always my face—my mother's thin eyebrows
and round arcs, my father's exclamation-point chin.
Each grey hair earned and earned and earned.
This year bends toward its end, another lion, another sum
of circulations around the sun. I take inventory
of this year's births: my children proliferated
from my hands—little letters, little seeds.
I kiss your eyelids, perfume my fingertips
with your fragrant leaves. Bless me, bless you—
across the wind, scattered and ever hopeful for blooming.

HERE

The doves wake us in the morning.
Here, we wake to greet seeds,
tiny beginnings, waking in tiny trays,
little first houses we've made for them
in this first home we're making together.
Always, in a new place, I wonder how
I've gotten here. I think on the mirrors
I could look through the past into—
the flat noses and crinkled eyes and brown skin
that lived and lived and lived so that I could live
this life. Was I a seed in the eye of my mother
before she met my father? Was she a seed
in my grandmother's eye, my grandmother
before she was made to marry a man
she did not love? *The Japanese are coming.*
You are a third daughter. He wants you.
He will take care of you. Better a wife than
a dead girl. Better a wife than a mistress;
better a mother than an old maid; better a poor
woman with too many children than a woman
alone. In this country, in this countryside,
the wind carries my thoughts across the valley
over the mountains, eastward over the continent
I drove across with another man I loved whose
anger (or sadness? or hate?) was a seed buried
in what I thought was love. I ran and ran and ran
away from him when I woke beside him: a woman
alone. The dirt and dust of that house became a mask
I couldn't wash away and when I ran all the loose change
and receipts and answers flew from my pockets and
scattered onto the highway. And now, years later,
a new life with a different man who is not new, but
whose love is new in that it is discovered, as in I did
not know it could exist. And in the morning the doves

wake us to find each other first with our limbs, without the help of our eyes, and what seeds wait there? What will push dirt aside and bloom now and many years from now?

Q&A

Where are you from?

Two green coconuts
hatched inside muscle cars
not made for but driven in the snow.
They made a home from four beige walls
and covered it in wooden forks and spoons.

Oh, OK. But, where are your parents from?

an acre of fertile land given up to God;
an emptying mahjong table; a grove of dropping lansones;
rice with patis without money for fish;
the slop of pig farms, the sway of beekeeper's veils;
pillows of pink granite, concrete angels covered in snow;
plastic tablecloths and plastic jugs of white vinegar;
the long song of continental drift; a widening ocean away.

But, where are you really from?

The karaoke song I cannot sing.
The last cigarette I keep smoking.
The one day I will write down the important list
of the important things, neatly and all by myself,
onto sad yellow legal pads, lined in blue.

POST DIASPORA

Elsewhere, butterflies mean something
I cannot remember—luck or life
or death or maybe it depends on
where the fluttering wings appear.
How exhausting (or dangerous)
to forget always what means what
where. *How do you say butterfly?*
Alitaptap? Tutubi? Or is that
dragonfly? Or *lighting bug?*
How do you say *I'm sorry* or *I miss you*
or *I don't know how not to forget?*

  •

Today's wonder: a river that begins
straight up from the ground as if
from nowhere. The trees around it ask—
but, *where were you born?*
Ultimately, which means more?
The seed's first wink? Or the root's first tip-toe?
Parents speak of before: *when you were but*
a twinkle in your father's eye. What hope
is born from the dust of those stars.

  •

There's a saying: those who do not swim
deep in the waters from which they came
cannot arrive in the oceans they hope to go.
My parents began an ocean away
and arrived in a land of lakes and snow.
I've been back to their water (is it mine, too?)
but, wasn't a good swimmer.

Everyone spoke underwater; I could only
hold my breath to listen for so long.
I did learn the water carries its own song.

•

The discipline of joy is about survival.
You make your own joy—
this is the work my mother taught me.
Little factory, little mine of reminders—
find, make, joy to sustain multiple life-
times: the blanket made beautiful
from patterned found scraps;
the broth of tap water and ginger and bones.
What fullness my mother earned
and could stuff inside an envelope
to send each month back home.

•

We all carry flags
whether we mean to
or not. I've grown more and more
suspicious of nation-
hood, the more and more I've had to
explain my face. I always had
a tough time with placing
my hand over my heart.
Holding it in my palm
was what my parents taught me.

•

My mother says: *You are a happy person.*
Write poems that show that.

I think she worries
my anger is a reflection
of where she went wrong.
I don't know how to
make her understand my anger
is a gift that she gave me.
Years of her gazing at the ground,
years of her prayer so that I could
decide to believe or not;
to use my mouth or keep it shut.

.

My mother proofreads my LinkedIn.
Are you stalking me on the internet,
ma? I text an emoji after so she knows
I'm mostly kidding. She sends me a
prayer given to the children of Fatima
by the Virgin Mary. We text this way
when talking makes us sigh or cry
with what we don't know. Too much
unsaid pinches beneath everything
we utter—our *modus operandi*—
I love you: you disappoint me: I love
you: you expect too much: I love you:
I say aloud all the wrong
words: I love you.

.

There are debts we carry
inside our insides—
debts that live in the spleen,
the liver, the stomach, the heart.
I think I carry my debts
owed my mother
inside my teeth, which have been
bound and corrected and polished

and whitened, year after year.
My mother's mouth is full
of white teeth and pink gums
made in a lab, made many years
after the loss of her own born smile.

•

Absence is what took me
so long to name after many years
of scrying the world for answers:
Why does this hollow live
inside my aching throat?
When the anemone's kisses cling
to my fingertips, what does it mourn?
What is my mother's greatest fear
and my father's last legacy?

UPON REREADING *ISLAND OF THE BLUE DOLPHINS*

I remember the ache—
to hunt for devilfish
and live among the sea elephants;
to gather abalone
and sharpen my arrows and hooks
by the light of tiny, slow-burning silver fish;
to weave yucca and tend to my own home
of kelp and whale bones.
I wanted my own wilderness,
a blanket to wrap around myself.
The relief of solitude,
the salve of animals as my only company.
I learned an otter would not withhold its affection,
would only offer its belly
to your offers of fish.
I wanted to be the last of my people,
a girl without
mother, father, sister, brother—
a girl belonging to no one,
my only belongings a cormorant skirt
and a cage of tiny birds.
My only family the wild dog
that killed my brother—
the wild dog I could not kill
and so fed and tamed and named.

NOTES

"Former Possessions of the Spanish Empire" refers to the *Catálogo alfabético de apellidos*, a book of surnames published in 1849 after Spanish Governor-General Narciso Clavería y Zaldúa issued a decree to address the lack of standard naming convention, in order for Spain to effectively collect taxes in the Philippines.

The epigraph for "Pioneer" comes from Bernard Heuvelmans who wrote *Sur la Piste des Bêtes Ignorées* (*On the Track of Unknown Animals*) and is regarded as a founding figure in cryptozoology, the search for and study of animals whose existence or survival is disputed or unsubstantiated, such as the Loch Ness monster and the yeti.

Understanding the Filipino was written by Tomas D. Andres and Pilar Corazón B. Ilada-Andrés. In their preface, they state: "This book is a detailed study of Filipino etiquette, values, mores, customs and manners which show the differences as well as similarities in behavioral expectations that arise when a Westerner comes to live in an Eastern culture."

"This Is Not A Gentle Poem" takes its title from a line in Arne Pihl's poem, "Here," displayed in reflective vinyl on four 12 feet long and 8 feet tall plinths at Denny Way, as part of ALL RISE, a series of temporary art installations at the location of Seattle City Light's future Denny Substation.

"When Will We Ache Less" quotes, as reported by the *New York Times* alongside several other major news outlets, several hundred torch-bearing white nationalists, who marched on the main quadrangle of the University of Virginia's grounds and through the streets of Charleston, South Carolina, shouting, "You will not replace us" and "Jews will not replace us."

"Lava" is for KC and Tessa.

The images in "Daguerreotype" are indebted to the work
and words of the artist Binh Danh, particularly his projects,
"Ancestral Altars" and "In the Eclipse of Angkor."

"Payatas" is for Ate Susan, Ate Ged, and Kim McGlynn.

"Post Diaspora" began from participating in "Because We
Come From Everything: Poetry & Migration," a postcard
project through Kundiman and the Poetry Coalition.

"Tabi Tabi, Po" is for Chaney.

"Here" is for my lola, my mother, and Alex.

ACKNOWLEDGMENTS

My gratitude to the editors, staff, and readers of the publications in which these poems—sometimes in different form—first appeared:

Asian American Literary Review: "Patterns of Love in People of Diaspora," "In Dreams, The Dead Sing," "My Father On the Line." *Bellingham Review*: "Thread Rite," "Letter From My Mother." *Birmingham Poetry Review*: "Night Fishing," "On Migration, Upon Finding an Old Map." *The Cincinnati Review*: "Q&A [Where are you from?]." *The Collagist*: "Proverbial." *Hyphen*: "Family Kundiman," "Daguerreotype." *Jack Straw*: "To The Older Couple Also Eating Dunkin' Donuts at O'Hare." *Lantern Review*: "Vestige." *The Margins*: "Nostalgia is a Dangerous Thing," "Upon Rereading Island of the Blue Dolphins." *Meritage Press*: "Butiki." *Moss*: "When Will We Ache Less." *Mythium*: "Transgression," "Magsaysay Drive, Olongapo City: Nawa Sa Pagsasalin." *Nashville Review*: "Late Afternoon with Chagall." *New England Review*: "When My Mother Was Eartha Kitt," "This Is Not a Gentle Poem." *The Nervous Breakdown*: "Payatas." *The Normal School*: "Tabi Tabi, Po," "We Are So Sorry For Your Lost." *Okey-Pankey / Electric Literature*: "Desire," "Constellation." *Pleiades*: "A Strange Constellation of Desires." *Poetry Northwest*: "I Read the Signs," "Lava." *Prairie Schooner*: "Variations on Prayer and the Color Brown," "Post Diaspora." *Third Coast*: "Q&A [Who would invent the egg?]." *ROAR*: "Pioneer," "Partial." *Upstreet*: "Here." *Vinyl*: "Former Possessions of the Spanish Empire."

"Thread Rite," "My Father, On the Line" and "Letter to My Mother" appeared in the anthology, *Two Countries: U.S. Daughters & Sons of Immigrant Parents* (Red Hen Press, 2017).

Additionally, a few of these poems also appeared in the chapbooks, *landscape/heartbreak* (Two Sylvias, 2015) and *Last Night I Dreamt of Volcanos* (Organic Weapon Arts, 2015).

Thank you, Valerie Wallace and Megan Gravendyk-Estrella, for honoring my book with the 2018 National Hillary Gravendyk Prize, and giving it a home. Thank you, Cati Porter, for making it a wonderful home.

Thank you to Garrett Hongo, Aimee Nezhukhumatathil, and Barbara Jane Reyes for your generous welcome and remarkably kind words.

Thank you, Roberto Jamora, for sharing your painting (salamat, kapatid!) for this cover. Thank you, Kenji Liu for the beautiful cover and book design.

Thank you, Quenton Baker, Bill Carty, Meghan Dunn, Jessa Heath, Tessa Hulls, Matthew Schnirman, and Jane Wong, for your invaluable feedback on this collection.

To friends, fellow writers, and teachers at the University of Oregon, Richard Hugo House, Jack Straw Writers Program, Bread Loaf Writers' Conference, Napa Valley Writers' Conference, VONA Voices, and the Key West Literary Seminar—thank you for community, resources and support.

To 4Culture, Artist Trust, Oregon Literary Arts and Philippine American Writers and Artists (PAWA), thank you for the financial resources that supported the writing of these poems.

To Vermont Studio Center, Artsmith, Centrum, Lemon Tree House, and Caldera—thank you for the time, resources, and beautiful spaces in which to work.

Special thanks the following folks who helped along and inspired many of these poems: Aimee Suzara, Anastacia Reneé Tolbert, Arlene Kim, Arlo Voorhees, Arthur Sze, Cathy Linh Che, Chaney Kwak, Dan Lau, Daphne Stanford, David Mura, Devon Midori Hale, Eddie Kim, Ellen Bryant Voigt, Eric John Olson, Ged Hidalgo, Keith Leonard, Keith Wilson, Kim McGlynn, Laurel Fantauzzo, Mary Koles, Matthew Olzmann,

Melanie Noel, Natasha Trethewey, Nikki Zielinski, Oliver de la Paz, Rick Barot, Susan Quimpo, Tarfia Faizullah, and Tarn MacArthur.

To Kate Daniels, for opening my first (official) door to poetry. To Lawson Fusao Inada, for writing back. Thank you.

To Shefali Lal, Alison Piepmeier, and Tina Chen—for your generosity; for believing (and helping me to believe) in my power to create. Thank you, thank you, thank you.

To Geri Doran, for prompts and patience, thank you.

To Garrett Hongo, for wisdom and impatience; for pushing me (and pushing me!), always—thank you.

To Kundiman, for the beacon and the home. Thank you.

To my magical, rural community—for showing me what it means to grow your living from the ground that bears your weight. Thank you.

To Jonterri Gadson, roommate, soulmate. To Ula Janik, a friend (a pal and a confidante). To Douglas Tsoi, for all the (pictures of) food. Thank you.

To my raccoon sistren, to whom I raise my own strange paws— Jane Wong and Tessa Hulls—thank you for the ferocity of your love and friendship.

To Catherine Clepper, Emily Emerson, and Natalie Gualy, for over twenty years (!) of encouragement and love. Thank you.

To my beautiful, multitudinous family—in the US and the Philippines—for your myriad forms of support and love, for your faith and stories and laughter, for being my first teachers in the music of language. For teaching me the many ways to be strong. Salamat. Love, and thank you, always.

Special salamat to Tito Rofel, for paving the way for poets in the family.

Finally, and most of all, to my mother and father—I love you. For every sacrifice, for my lucky and beautiful life, for everything—thank you. Your love was my first and most important lesson.

And, Alex. My favorite person. I love you.

Michelle Peñaloza was born in the suburbs of Detroit, Michigan and grew up in the suburbs of Nashville, Tennessee. She is the author of two chapbooks, *landscape/heartbreak* (Two Sylvias, 2015), and *Last Night I Dreamt of Volcanoes* (Organic Weapon Arts, 2015). *Former Possessions of the Spanish Empire*, winner of the 2018 Hillary Gravendyk National Poetry Prize, is her debut full-length collection. Her poems appear in *Prairie Schooner, New England Review, TriQuarterly, Pleiades, Electric Literature, Poetry Northwest*, and other journals and anthologies. A Kundiman fellow, she is the recipient of the Starlin Poetry Prize from the University of Oregon, grants from Artist Trust and 4Culture, as well as fellowships and scholarships from VONA/Voices, Oregon Literary Arts, the Richard Hugo House, Lemon Tree House, Caldera, the Bread Loaf Writers' Conference, and the Key West Literary Seminar, among others. Michelle lives in rural Northern California.

ABOUT THE HILLARY GRAVENDYK PRIZE

The Hillary Gravendyk Prize is an open poetry book competition published by Inlandia Institute for all writers regardless of the number of previously published poetry collections.

HILLARY GRAVENDYK (1979-2014) was a beloved poet living and teaching in Southern California's "Inland Empire" region. She wrote the acclaimed poetry book, *HARM* from Omnidawn Publishing (2012) and the poetry collection *The Naturalist* (Achiote Press, 2008). A native of Washington State, she was an admired Assistant Professor of English at Pomona College in Claremont, CA. Her poetry has appeared widely in journals such as *American Letters & Commentary, The Bellingham Review, The Colorado Review, The Eleventh Muse, Fourteen Hills, MARY, 1913: A Journal of Forms, Octopus Magazine, Tarpaulin Sky* and *Sugar House Review.* She was awarded a 2015 Pushcart Prize for her poem "Your Ghost," which appeared in the Pushcart Prize Anthology. She leaves behind many devoted colleagues, friends, family and beautiful poems. Hillary Gravendyk passed away on May 10, 2014 after a long illness. This contest has been established in her memory.

ABOUT INLANDIA INSTITUTE

Inlandia Institute is a regional non-profit and literary center. We seek to bring focus to the richness of the literary enterprise that has existed in this region for ages. The mission of the Inlandia Institute is to recognize, support, and expand literary activity in all of its forms in Inland Southern California by publishing books and sponsoring programs that deepen people's awareness, understanding, and appreciation of this unique, complex and creatively vibrant region.

The Institute publishes books, presents free public literary and cultural programming, provides in-school and after school enrichment programs for children and youth, holds free creative writing workshops for teens and adults, and boot camp intensives. In addition, every two years, the Inlandia Institute appoints a distinguished jury panel from outside of the region to name an Inlandia Literary Laureate who serves as an ambassador for the Inlandia Institute, promoting literature, creative literacy, and community. Laureates to date include Susan Straight (2010-2012), Gayle Brandeis (2012-2014), Juan Delgado (2014-2016), Nikia Chaney (2016-2018), and Rachelle Cruz (2018-2020).

To learn more about the Inlandia Institute, please visit our website at www.InlandiaInstitute.org.

OTHER HILLARY GRAVENDYK PRIZE BOOKS

All the Emergency-Type Structures by Elizabeth Cantwell
Winner of the 2018 Regional Hillary Gravendyk Prize

Our Bruises Kept Singing Purple by Malcolm Friend
Winner of the 2017 National Hillary Gravendyk Prize

Traces of a Fifth Column by Marco Maisto
Winner of the 2016 National Hillary Gravendyk Prize

God's Will for Monsters by Rachelle Cruz
Winner of the 2016 Regional Hillary Gravendyk Prize
Winner of a 2018 American Book Award

Map of an Onion by Kenji C. Liu
Winner of the 2015 National Hillary Gravendyk Prize

All Things Lose Thousands of Times by Angela Peñaredondo
Winner of the 2015 Regional Hillary Gravendyk Prize

CPSIA information can be obtained
at www.ICGtesting.com
Printed in the USA
LVHW041926301019
635835LV00006B/1014/P